Ottawa-Our Nation's Capital

Ottawa~Our Nation's Capital

Photographs by
RUDI HAAS

•

Introduction by
COLLEEN ANDERSON KONG

Toronto
OXFORD UNIVERSITY PRESS
1980

My thanks are due to those who helped to make this book possible,
in particular Mr and Mrs Tom Wood; Mr and Mrs Paul von Baich;
Mr and Mrs Dominick Sarsfield; and Roger Boulton.   R.H.

Jacket photograph: the Parliament Buildings from Nepean Point

Designed by *Fortunato Aglialoro*

©Oxford University Press (Canadian Branch) 1980
ISBN 0-19-540340-1
1 2 3 4-2 1 0 9
Printed in Hong Kong by
EVERBEST PRINTING COMPANY LIMITED

Introduction
by Colleen Anderson Kong

At dawn, uniformed guards stretch after their night-watch, fasten their lunch-boxes and trot off to catch the bus, oblivious of limousines with diplomatic plates on their way to the airport.

Ignoring the formidable statues of historic figures, waitresses rush to work across Confederation Square. Among the contemporary sculptures in downtown parks, birdwatchers stalk wildlife, from waxwings to Royal Swans.

On top of the National Arts Centre, security staff, like archers on a Norman fortress, prepare for yet another state visit; while down the road at Byward Market, shopkeepers set up their stalls for another market day.

Later the museums come to life—fourteen of them, including the National Museum of Man, the National Museum of Science and Technology, the National Gallery of Canada, with everything from a Depression-era prairie kitchen to the skis of Jackrabbit Johannson, at one hundred and twenty Canada's oldest cross-country skier.

Ottawa believes itself to be the Winter Capital of the World. This is not surprising, considering that it has nearly six dark months a year of lung-gripping temperatures and towering walls of wind-whipped snow. Yet the climate fails to discourage its citizens from claiming for Ottawa another distinction yet, as the Fitness Capital of the World.

The whole city abounds with outdoor activities on its winding cross-country ski trails, jogging and biking paths, nature trails, toboggan hills, snow-shoe areas, and ice-fishing spots–and the world's longest skating rink, the frozen waters of the Rideau Canal, winding through a magnificent setting in the heart of the city.

While half a million skaters enjoy this canal-rink every winter, the onlooker can watch the world skim by: babies hauled on sleighs, businessmen with briefcases skating to work, two Dutch regulars wearing hundred-year-old skates, ice-flying nuns, turbaned East Indians, toque-topped Africans floundering with helpless laughter.

In the spring, as crocuses brighten the melting snow and millions of daffodils and tulips come into bloom, the fitness fever rages on. Thousands of runners join the National Capital Marathon. As summer arrives and Ottawa swelters, everyone changes track suits for swim suits. Four city beaches, a twelve-hundred-acre agricultural research farm, Dow's Lake and one hundred and eighty parks fill with picnickers.

The site that was destined to be the capital of the second-largest nation in the world was known only as a stopover point on the canoe route from the St Lawrence to the hinterland until the end of the eighteenth century. Eastern Upper Canada was purchased from the Mississauga Indians in 1783. Townships were laid out ten years later and at the turn of the century Philemon Wright, a Puritan farmer from Massachusetts, came with a group of colonists to settle on the north shore (what is now Hull, Quebec) and built it into a thriving area for lumber and industry. In 1826 Lieutenant Colonel John By of the Royal Engineers arrived to plan the Rideau Canal, part of a system linking Montreal with Lake Ontario. He laid out two settlements, Upper and Lower Town, divided by Barracks Hill.

Between the lumbermen and canal labourers, the settlement became notorious for riots, violence, drunken brawling, and back-alley debauchery. Bytown grew into a sulphurous, fuming industrial centre.

Bytown was renamed Ottawa in 1855. (The name may be a distortion of Outaouais, or, some say, of the Indian word Adawe, meaning 'place-of-trade'.) It was chosen as the capital of the Province of Canada in 1857 and of the Dominion of Canada in 1867. While the rest of Canada scorned the new 'backwoods capital', Ottawa scrubbed her grimy face, groomed her manners, and emerged in the splendour befitting her lofty status—resplendent with Gothic revival, Scottish baronial, and Château-style architecture. Rowdy Barracks Hill became the site of the Parliament Buildings — the East and West Blocks and the original Centre Block, including the Library of Parliament — which was built in 1860-6. The Centre Block was destroyed by fire in 1916 (except for the Library) and rebuilt in a much-enlarged form in 1916-24. Containing the House of Commons and the Senate Chamber as well as the Library, it is adorned by the soaring Peace Tower (begun in 1919 and dedicated in 1927) that stands in front of it and is the focal point of the whole Parliament Hill complex. Today Ottawa glitters with waterways, scenic driveways and crisp modern architecture. Nowadays the only noticeable industry in Ottawa is the recycling of public servants.

Characteristic of Ottawa is the proliferation of copper roofs, weathered to a peculiar shade of green.

Also particularly Ottawan:

The cocktail party conversation: 'Look, there's François Boggs. He's just been promoted to an AS-4 with Stat-Can, and here comes Nigel Desjardins, an SX-1 with Ag-Can.'

Impatient skiers on skateboard skis, schussing through October leaves down the Gatineau Hills.

Our 'bilingual' street signs, in a lingo known as 'bling': Rue Bank St., Chem. Russell Rd., Prom. Queen Elizabeth Dr., Stop Arrêt.

The Byward Market, where our mostly French-Canadian market gardeners arrive at dawn to set up their street stalls with everything from dewy-fresh fruits and vegetables, honey, maple syrup, eggs, meat, trees, sod and flowers, to live fowl and rabbits.

The multiplicity of our culture, food, fashions and accents, reflecting that we are from everywhere but Ottawa. Rudi Haas, from Austria, and I, from rural Manitoba, are typical Ottawans who, when heading north on Colonel By Drive, reach the tableau of the Peace Tower, Conference Centre, Château Laurier, all rising above the canal, and always think with a sentimental rush of affection: 'Backwoods, eh? This is a great place to visit — an even better place to live.'

1   The Governor General's Foot
Guards in front of the Peace Tower

2   Tulips, Rockcliffe Park

3   Tulips, Vincent Massey Park

4 Dow's Lake

5   Brown's Inlet, by the Rideau Canal

(over) 6 Dow's Lake

7 The Rideau Canal at night, with silhouettes of the National Arts Centre (*left*), the Parliament Buildings, and the Conference Centre (*right*)

8   Parliament Hill, showing
silhouettes of the Peace Tower (*left*)
and the Library of Parliament (*right*)

9   Statue of Samuel de Champlain, Nepean Point

10 Marina in Hull
with Alexandra Bridge

11 Alexandra Bridge and the
Ottawa River, Hull

14 Hog's Back Falls, Rideau River

15 Swans on the Rideau River

16   Rideau River by Billings Bridge

17   Statue of Colonel By, builder
of the Rideau Canal, at Major's Hill
Park

JOHN BY
LT. COLONEL ROYAL ENG'RS

18　Statue of Queen Victoria on
Parliament Hill

19　National Arts Centre

20 The Café at the National Arts Centre, by the Rideau Canal

21 Sculpture by Daudelin at the National Arts Centre, with Place Bell
Canada in the background

(over)
22 National Arts Centre

23 Wing of Harvard MK II, Canadian War Museum

24 Place du Portage in Hull, Quebec

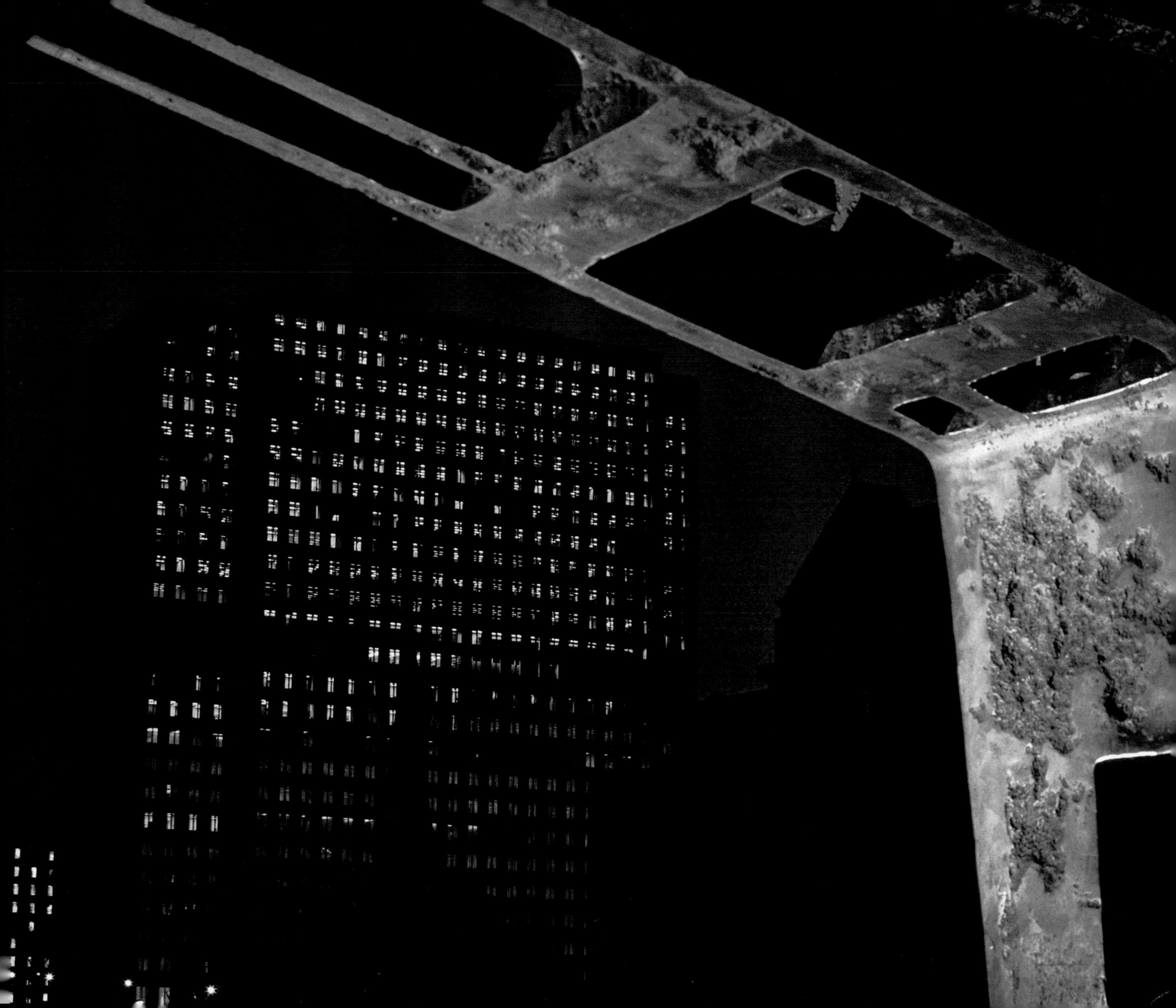

22   23

25 Wild sunflowers

26 Carleton University

27 Towers of Basilique Notre-Dame d'Ottawa—the oldest extant church in Ottawa (1816)—on Sussex Drive, with LaSalle Academy in the foreground

28 The Parliament Buildings from the east

29   Nuntiatura Apostolica, Manor Avenue, Rockcliffe

30 Earnscliffe, Sussex Drive. Once the home of Canada's first Prime
Minister, Sir John A. Macdonald, it is now the residence of the
British High Commissioner.

31 Island Park Drive

32   Rideau Canal

33 Byward Market

34 York Street, Byward Market area

35 Parc de la Gatineau, Quebec

36 Gatineau Hills by Wakefield

37 Farrellton, Quebec

38 Canadian dog-sled championships at Nepean Sportsplex

(over) 39 Farrellton, Quebec

40 Rideau Canal

41 Rideau Canal, with the Château Laurier in the background

42 A skater on the Rideau Canal

41

43   Warrington Drive

44   Rideau River Falls, with the Commonwealth Air Force Memorial
and the External Affairs building in the background

75 National Museum of Science and Technology

76 Dow's Lake

47   National Arts Centre

48   Central Chambers (built in 1890) on Elgin Street overlooking Confederation Square

(over)
49   Wakefield

50   Gatineau Hills

87   Sculpture at the base of the
Samuel de Champlain monument,
Nepean Point

84

51   Mont Ste-Marie

52   Mont Ste-Marie

53   Farrellton, Quebec

54 Manotick

55 Rideau River Drive

56 St Patrick Street

57   Sussex Drive — Clarence Street

58   Annual National Capital Marathon, Colonel By Drive

59 Bank and Wellington Streets

60 Sussex Drive, with the Parliament Buildings in the background

(over)

61 City Hall, Sussex Drive

62 Queen Elizabeth Driveway

61

62

63 Spring Festival, Rideau Canal

64 Spring Festival, Rideau Canal

65   Yukon Display, Canada Day Parade, Parliament Hill

66   Rideau Street

69 'Royal Highland Emigrants',
Canadian War Museum, Sussex Drive

70   Highland Games, Lansdowne Park

71   Spring Festival, Major's Hill Park

72   Spring Festival

73 Sparks Street Mall

74   Sparks Street Mall

75 National Museum of Science and Technology

76 Dow's Lake

77 Rideau River Falls

78 Hog's Back Falls, Rideau River

79　Rideau River Drive

81 Parliament Buildings from Major's Hill Park

(over)
83 Canada Day Parade, Parliament Hill. In the background is the Peace Tower, in front of the Centre Block of the Parliament Buildings, with the East Block on the right.

82 National Arts Centre

84 Celebration of 150th anniversary of the Rideau Canal

85 Wrought-iron crestings on the west roof of the East Block of the Parliament Buildings

86 Astrolabe Theatre, on Nepean Point, Ottawa River, with the Parliament Buildings in the background

87 Sculpture at the base of the
Samuel de Champlain monument,
Nepean Point